The Depth of Hidden Value

Author Sharee D. Strickland

DEDICATION PAGE

I dedicate this book to everyone who has something to say, but lacks the courage to reveal their true inner feelings.

I am not a scholar, nor do I have a Ph.D. I just have a story to tell about some of my experiences and what helped me get to a place of discovering who I am, hoping to encourage the voiceless.

Introduction

Merriam-Webster defines losing as "resulting in or likely to result in defeat." The word that sticks out the most to me is the word likely. What I have come to learn is that not everything that we lose is a loss. Some things we lose open the door for us to gain. On the other side of losing is winning. Every winner has endured a loss that has affected them a great deal while propelling them to something greater. This reminds me of the three championships the Chicago Bulls won from 1990-1993, then to lose two seasons in a row, and return with three NBA championships thereafter in the 1995-1998 seasons. The losses between the wins have a way of creating balance where there's imbalance. I say that because when you're winning, the thought of losing never crosses your mind. And when you lose, it's in that space where you're molded and who you truly are resurfaces.

Losing increases the probability for new opportunities and opens the door for greater possibilities. In the beginning stages of loss, a moment of reflection happens. It gives you time to reflect, regroup and start again. The goal is not to get stuck in the reflection stage for too long, because no progress happens when you are stuck.

After the Chicago Bulls failed to win the championship two seasons in a row, something phenomenal happened three consecutive years later. They returned to 3-peat, the coined statement that only Chi-Town feels and understands on a different level.

Through this, one can learn to embrace loss. One can become stronger. The time you spend rebuilding or regrouping, can push you to an even higher level than you were before those challenges events happened.

Acknowledgments

Thank you first to God, The Highest, for inspiring and instilling the thought to write this book and for providing me the positive mindset that I could do this. I give You all the glory and honor in advance.

Thank you to everyone who has encouraged me along the way, it truly means a lot to me. I am grateful for all of your congratulatory messages.

A special thank you to my mother, who encouraged me to the finish line and reinforced my faith in God to get it done. I love you, Momma.

Thank you God for my experiences and allowing the disappointments, discouragements, despair, persecution and embarrassments to be present. The downfalls inspired and pushed me to be better. They allowed me to see where I was missing the mark and where I needed the most improvement. Thank you God for stirring up the gift inside of me to share with the world. It was through those challenging instances throughout my life that shaped me to be who I am today.

The concept of writing this book occurred about five years ago when I recognized I had something to share with the world about who I was. Writing this book was my way of releasing some of the deepest events that affected me to my core—events that exposed and opened the door to hope for someone else. This was my outlet and it is important that I not only share it with the world, but it is my responsibility to help those who want to tell their story but feel hopeless.

Again, thank you to everyone who had a part in making my dream come true and I pray that God receives the increase.

Table of Contents

Dedication

Introduction

Acknowledgements

The Weight Loss

Being overweight can be a different type of obstacle for many. Some people are genetically overweight, while others are faced with underlying medical conditions and some people gradually gain excess weight over time. I'd been very petite most of my life; my mother would buy me new clothes and still would have to alter many of the pieces to fit me. Even after giving birth to my son, I only gained a small amount of weight. It wasn't until years later, after many years of neglect that I noticed such a drastic change in my appearance. I noticed my favorite jeans, I could no longer fit and the difficulty in zipping of my coat was obviously. Struggling and forcing my thick thighs into jeans, jumping, lying down on the bed; all to get them zipped and buttoned up.

I was in this strange space for almost three years, before I decided to do something about my weight and my health. I pretended I liked what I saw on the outside, but really I liked the idea of what I presented to the world: a levelheaded black woman, strong, chasing her dreams, successful, and accomplished. But this was all a façade. I didn't feel well and lacked energy. I was exhausted from the day's activities and the last thing I wanted to do was exercise. I wanted to have a meal and go to bed after a long day's work.

After many days and nights of going to bed and waking up the same way, I was ready to find an answer; a resolution to what I thought was a weight problem. I tried everything; I went to many local gyms, took a laundry list of classes at independent locations, and tried a few different types of diets. My favorite was the food topper sold on QVC. It came with two shakers, one for sweet foods and one for salty. The concept was to sprinkle the sweet blend on anything that would normally be sweet; the other was to be topped on anything that would normally be salty. The substance in the shakers was "supposed to" reverse your desire to eat, and gradually the meals would become smaller. QVC mastered the marketing on this; however, it sure as hell didn't make me want to stop eating. As a matter of fact, I did the exact opposite. I ate even *more*. My $20 investment was a $20 scam. Needless to say, none of these remedies worked for me. I continued to try to work out on my own at a local gym, only to see my weight wasn't fluctuating after months of going in the gym.

I'd been struggling for a long time. After several repeated doctor's visits, with my doctor reminding me that I wasn't taking care of myself, encouraging me to make productive changes for my health and wellness. I heard what she said, but I wasn't fully listening.

Time passed, and while my health was declining, the numbers on the scale were climbing. I reached a low point of depression and embarrassment that frustrated me even more. I didn't quite understand what was happening to me.

There was a state of loss where I knew something was wrong. At this time in my life I decided to do something different, something that would change the rest of my life. I made a conscience decision that I was tired of the way I was living. I didn't like what I saw when I looked in the mirror, my clothes didn't fit and I was uncomfortable. The people I'd meet on a regular basis had no idea of my inner struggles because I hid it so well…or so I thought. But what I'd come to realize was, no matter what picture I painted to the world, being true and honest with myself was what truly mattered.

I could dress myself up in the finest attire, get my hair done up, and my makeup all in place. But one thing was certain…I could never hide from myself. My inner struggles eventually manifested itself outward with every relationship I shared. Who we truly are as a person, will surface at the least opportune time. When I should have been my best, I wasn't because at the time I couldn't.

At this time in my life, Facebook and social media were on the rise. As I was learning my way around Facebook, I saw a video of a fitness class. What better place to learn how to do something than being on social media, right? I clicked on the pre-recorded video of the fitness class. The patrons were in sync; the music was playing; the people were screaming, smiling, and sweating all at the same time. I couldn't help but notice the upbeat trainer and owner of the facility. I'd seen a ton of workout videos in my time, but this trainer provided an overload of energy and enthusiasm, having the entire class engaged. Not one person was sitting on the sideline.

It was inspirational. Participants seemed to be having fun, and the energy in the class was over-the-top crazy. I watched the entire video and by the end, every person was dripping with sweat and those that could move did; everyone else had to take a break. I noticed the trainer would take a group picture of the team after each workout. I immediately thought to myself, *this is not your typical workout class.* It was more like athletes in training. I'd never witnessed a workout class like this before.

After watching one video, I continued to view a few more and finally took the leap of faith. I messaged the location a few times but was unable to connect with a trainer. I decided to call the facility and a trainer answered the phone on the first ring. It was the owner, and when I heard his voice, my nerves kicked in and I wanted to hang up on him but I decided not to. The trainer answered the phone with exhaustion and energy in his tone, you could tell he'd just finished a class, I told him I'd seen him on Facebook and explained my fitness struggles, and He calmly listened. After explaining my story to the trainer, He convinced me to come out a class.

While I was making classic holiday dinner, loaded with calories, unhealthy and yet tasteful choices, I left to go to the class and give it a try. I walked in feeling shy and a little afraid at the same time. Everyone in the class seemed to be smiling; most were in good shape or well on their way to achieving their fitness goals.

I had no idea what I was in for. There were

many women who seemed to be engulfed in fitness, dripping with sweat, and the smell of perspiration filled the air. I thought, *well, if you leave now, you can get home and prepare your next dish for the holiday.* But before I could turn around, the trainer approached me and he was not the calm guy I talked to on the phone. This high energy, loud, enthusiastic man came from around the corner. After he explained the workout, I was thinking even more to myself, *Girl leave now...you don't have to be here.* But I stayed.

I found a secluded spot in the back of the room, out of the way, hoping I was hiding from everyone else. The workout started, and I found myself on the floor in about three minutes. Now that I think of it, I spent most of the time on the floor. I literally thought I was dying. As I gasped for air, out of breath, sweating profusely, gazing up from the floor on my hands and knees, while I watched everyone else continue to work out, it was in that moment my window of opportunity presented itself. I made a conscious decision that would change the rest of my entire life. In that very second, I challenged myself, which opened the door to the next chapter for me. What this taught me was while I didn't have the answers to my problems, they would eventually come if I took the first step.

For four weeks I didn't lose a pound—well, technically, I lost three pounds, but my trainer reminded me that wasn't an accomplishment nor worth celebrating. I was heartbroken after the conversation. However, what I learned was that I had to be committed, if I wanted to lose weight and lead a healthy lifestyle; I had to be disciplined, dedicated and follow the plan. There were no shortcuts to fitness and wellness.

Discipline, dedication, and screaming pep talks from my trainer and I was down almost ten pounds. I felt ecstatic! I finally found a rhythm with my meal plan and exercise regimen. At this point, I felt better than I'd felt in many years…physically. As I stood in front of my mirror, admiring my small yet noticeable progression, I smiled at my reflection. I thought about what workout clothes I was going to wear and what I was going to eat for the day.

I continued to lose weight—totaling 30 pounds in three months. Thirty pounds brought me down to 123 pounds. I couldn't remember the last time I saw that number on the scale. I just knew it had been a very long time.

I became motivation for many people on their fitness journeys and I was often complimented on my weight loss. Many people would contact me and ask for help as if I had a secret solution. But I didn't. I had just become focused on losing weight and eating better. The more I focused, the more I lost, and the better I looked to the people looking at me. I finally liked what I saw physically when I looked in the mirror and I couldn't imagine not hearing the compliments, even though they gave me a false sense of esteem about myself.

I began to live in fitness facilities; I had gym memberships all over the place. I became so addicted to the feeling attached to working out that I began to neglect even more things in my life while pouring myself into working out.

After working out in the facility for some time, having what I thought was a good grasp on my fitness goals, I learned to control my meals as well as the basics of training, and I left the facility to work out on my own. I continued to work out and my weight fluctuated. During this time away from the workout facility I became more in tune with myself. I'd crossed one hurdle in life that I thought was impossible.

Losing weight and building a better, healthier me grew me closer to what I thought was self-confidence. It taught me that it's okay to trust myself. After overcoming this challenge, I felt there was still something missing. I'd gained control of my health, but I couldn't quite figure it out. I looked good, I felt good physically, but I didn't know what it was. What I did know is that I still wasn't happy. I was still sad after such a huge achievement. Who wouldn't be happy about such a feat?

I came to discover I had some broken pieces and needed to understand what those were. I was a broken vessel, and while exercising and eating properly was the right thing for me to do; I needed to be healed on the inside. My physical weight was not the only excess baggage. I had emotional weight issues. I just didn't know how to lose it. See emotional weight isn't measured on the scale, it's manifested in your appearance, your outward behavior, and how you feel on the inside. Emotional weight can't be exercised away in the gym or covered up by wearing a waist trainer.

"You can't judge me; I judge myself enough."

The Mask

Loss, or the act of losing, can feel like something is being removed or taken from you without your approval – Simply snatched from you in the blink of an eye, with no warning. For me, loss felt like someone had stolen something from me and I didn't have   the opportunity to get it back.

During the process of loss, our body, mind, and soul can experience a series of scenarios and processes. While the mind is in overdrive, trying to sort through and understand what occurred, the body can feel as if it wants to shut down. The body no longer has the encouragement it needs from the mind to function properly. And while the soul is left to deal on its own, it accepts whatever the universe throws its way to sooth or ease the pain of the actual loss. This behavior mirrored what exercising did for me.

My mind was not ready for the abundance of sudden life changes. The mind is designed to direct and provide options to make decisions. When traumatic events occur, the events can send our mind into complete mental chaos. Without a good sense of control within our own lives, thoughts enter our minds - directing us either into a place of promotion or demotion. Having control of this mind space before a loss or sudden change presents itself into our lives, one can rise above the challenges when they arise making it easier to adjust to the situation accordingly. That doesn't mean you accept the loss immediately, but it can allows you to put your life and thoughts in better perspective.

This was my problem. I was not in control before the life changing events occurred, nor did I have a clue of where to start. I was not ready for the adjustments that came my way. My own thoughts often derailed me because I did not have control before the tragedies, before the challenges, or before the disappointments. I was in a place where I was not making clear and sound decisions in life; as a result of emotional trauma I was operating only on the surface—what's on the outside, what the world could see, and the tangible.

Do you know anyone like this and if so, how does what they show you relate to their behaviors? They seem to be winning in life but secretly struggling in areas not visible to many. Their families seem to be well taken care of, have awesome careers and display a happy lifestyle that some dream of The lifestyle and what happens secretly, should marry in some way; creating and displaying balance. The lack of balance in one's life; finds a way of displaying itself outwardly. And what I've come to learn from my own experiences, the lack of balance can easily be identified by someone else. While the concern is not on the surface, misguided thoughts eventually alter our direction and affect every person we come in contact with. Emotional trauma can alter and dictate a person's actions based on how you function or have the ability to cope with a traumatic event.

They say the first step to recovery is realizing there is a problem. A deep-rooted one at that. But what happens when you do know there is a problem but can't quite put your finger on it? After the realization - then comes denial once again. I was denying the fact that I truly had a concern, a problem, or an issue that needed to be addressed.

Instead, I learned to mask my problems with what I called success. I worked so much overtime, became a slave to work and personal relationships suffered. I suppose I was addicted to the money. People at work referred to me as dedicated or passionate. I started getting tired of being on call seven days a week, waking up in the middle of the night for emergencies, and being available every time my job needed me, while never being there for myself or my family.

I would work out in the gym every single day—I became a gym rat. I signed up for almost every fitness experience that I could. From swimming to CrossFit to H.I.T. to yoga… eventually that became exhausting.

Everything seemed to be coming together. I had a nice place to live, a nice car, and my son was off to college. Rising early on the weekends before my neighbors, out and about running errands, back home by noon. Anyone on the outside looking in probably thought my life was great.

There weren't too many things I wanted that I couldn't buy or somehow obtain. If I wanted it, I always found a way to get it. I preferred the quality of things and not the quantity. I was never flashy but always tried to shine and I never wanted what everyone else had.

I always wanted to be the exact opposite from what everyone else was. And for some reason, I liked the feeling of knowing I could make people dislike me. It's like that adrenaline rush you get after going on a roller coaster at a theme park.

But this was all a disguise for what was really going on inside of me. A mask covering up the real problem. You know what mask I'm talking about— the one that deflects the real issues and creates the façade for others to see. The outside looks good but you're really struggling on the inside. I could provide for my child but in some ways, I neglected what we truly needed. I had the ability to take care of myself in such a way that no one could tell I had serious problems.

"Train your mind to surpass how you feel."

Losing in Love

It was my birthday and I wanted to travel out of the country to celebrate my milestone birthday I'd traveled to many places but this time I wanted to celebrate my big day in another country. I contacted my travel agent, gave her my thoughts and she easily booked me a beautiful trip to an island... The sun, food, beautiful water, festivities and the vibe was amazing. One of my good friends joined me to celebrate; this was a trip I'd never forget. My travel agent advised me to be careful and I told her, "I'll be fine, I'm a big girl." I had no idea what I was in for.

The sights of pink sand beaches, indulging in island rum, conch salad and no worries for the next four days. After a couple of days of being on the trip, I went to a shindig where the locals from the island hung out. The energy was amazing with the sounds of the junkanoo band and people of all ages joining in on the fun, enjoying the cultured activities. Many storefronts and restaurants were lined up along the strip. There were so many it was difficult to decide which one to visit first. While in the thick of my evening at the fish fry, having the most fun on a trip ever, I was approached by a man with a strong accent, respectful and easy on the eyes. He asked my name and shook my hand. I told him my name, and he told me his.

While I did not come to the island to meet anyone, meeting new friends seemed harmless. I planned this trip to enjoy my birthday and create wonderful memories for years to come; I thought what harm could it be. In the midst of enjoying my evening, I realized but didn't give it much thought, the gentleman happened to be in my vicinity the entire evening, lurking. He never went away. Every time I turned around, he was right there, always in arms reach. My friend and I decided to stop along the way of enjoying our evening for a bite to eat. I decided on red snapper, rice, and peas. We shared the meal because there was too much food on the plate for just one person (delicious food and the seasoning was impeccable). The same guy appeared again as my friend and I waited for our meal; along the walking path of the outside restaurant. I ended up talking to him while my friend and I finished our meal. I felt I'd neglected my friend but I think she enjoyed watching me socialize and blush at the same time.

The conversation flowed so freely. I felt like I knew him already. We talked about everything— from the weather to children to the government. You name it, we discussed it. He asked me if I was single. I told him I was and asked him his status, of which he admitted he was single as well. Before leaving, we exchanged numbers and before the next night would come, he called me. I answered the phone and explained to him I'd call him back after I returned back to the States, but then things unraveled a bit.

After a couple weeks I contacted him. I had no idea this would be one of the most emotionally draining experiences I had ever experienced in my life. Conversations turned from minutes to hours. Hours turned to days. Conversations became more in depth. We talked about some of our dreams and aspirations, things we wanted to accomplish short and long term. We talked about an array of topics that went from one extreme to the next... The conversations were quite intriguing to hear from another's perspective how differently things are from the United States.

After the short butterfly stage ended, eventually, I noticed he didn't have many things to elaborate on. He listened to me talk about my dreams and what I saw as success, but never appended any of his own thoughts, ideas or imaginations; without being probed. After about three months, even with little to add, I was yet interested in getting to know this guy. He followed the same emotions by duplicating my responses, but in a different way.

After four months, I decided to take a trip back to see him and stayed for about a week. At that point for some reason I still was yet interested in this person and wanted to know more about him, plus I had the opportunity to see the beautiful island yet again. That was a win for me. Thereafter, we conversed some more, and he came to visit me in the States to meet my family, and if things worked out in the time allotted, we would continue dating.

I enjoyed his time while he was in the States. He could cook, he was domestic...there was nothing he couldn't do that I asked of him. I thought it was so attractive. It came time for him to return to his home country, I was emotional to say the least. I'd enjoyed our time together and looked forward to the next time I'd see him. He planned to return home to work with a plan to come back shortly after and we could continue our plan the future, at least that was what I believed. Six months later, he still had not yet returned.

Conversations and phone calls became intermittent. **Conflict arose,** and I'd become disturbed and promises were frequently broken. By this time, the frustration and anger were at an all-time high, but I was too emotionally invested at this point to just end things.

When he finally returned, my emotions were scattered all over the place. I was upset, but I also wanted him to be there. Every day was a struggle. The tension was so thick; you could have cut it with a knife. After two short weeks, he returned home. I thought to myself again, *I am a good catch, I am independent, and I have a lot going for myself, why am I wasting my time in this situation that doesn't make me happy? How did I allow this to happen to me? And what is it about this person that allowed me to remove the standards I thought I had for myself?*

Here, I found myself at an emotional crossroad. Asking myself why did I stay connected to someone that didn't yield a fulfillment. What I found was that it wasn't worth the tradeoff. Everyone desires to be with someone who adds and doesn't take away. I didn't get that from him, and I had to understand why. After months and months of back and forth, uncomfortable conversations, this relationship ended. I learned some things about myself. Not only did I undervalue myself, but I also completely dropped my standards. I'd come to the realization that some people aren't worth the time, energy, and sacrifices that manifest when being in a relationship. Learning to leave the table when the plate is clean was a bought lesson. Many times in life situations and circumstances give us hints, which provide direction. Ignoring the signs will not remove the reality of the circumstances. Pretending there isn't an elephant in the room, will not make the elephant disappear. Accepting the reality for what it really is, rather than attempting to dictate the outcome can prevent one from exhausting themselves mentally and emotionally. All of the signs were present, that this person was not for me, but the "need to know why" in me, would not allow me to accept the reality. Move on the moment you recognize your expectations or desires will not be met. Human nature can sometimes cause us to behave in ways we know go against our self-respect, values and essentially disregard our morals.

"My sanity is non-negotiable."

Mind Fucked

I had everything I thought I wanted. I'm a strong black woman and I can handle anything, I'm superwoman. That's what I told myself.

I would think things like *why doesn't everybody have the same work ethic as me? It's like everybody is lazy and wants absolutely nothing out of their lives. Why does everyone move so slowly? What about your future, don't you want more for yourself than you have right now?*

I had everything I wanted in life so why was I still struggling? I had absolutely no patience. I continued on with my life while going back and forth with myself in my head, praying to God, trying to understand where to pick up the pieces. *I'm good, keep doing what you're doing girl. They just don't understand,* is what I told myself. *Something is wrong but I don't want to be bothered right now.* I was wishy-washy and often back and forth and indecisive with my own thinking.

My life circumstances created a demon that only I had the power to destroy with God Almighty at my side. Everybody kept telling me, "You're a Christian, you know how to pray. Talk to God about it," or "Everything is going to be okay." But it wasn't. My faith and growing up a Christian from the age of three helped me to understand that I needed more than myself to get over this hump. Being a woman of faith with constant growth as a Christian helped me realize that I had many areas in my life where I needed development. I was prepared to handle on my own.

There are times people forget that Christians are human beings and not superheroes with special powers. We live, eat, breathe, and have meltdowns, too, just like everyone else. We are expected to exist as if everything is all right when many times it's all wrong. But thank God for Jesus because he revealed direction to me at this point. I needed God to show up and show out in my life, because I was fooling myself into thinking I was okay, when really I was mind fucked, confused, and mentally drained from the fraudulent person I'd become to myself. I wanted to be authentic to everyone else I encountered, but not to myself, creating the biggest conflict one could have…with self. Denying my own self and fulfilling the pleasures of those around me, only to find myself in a true deficit. Self-love was absent; I cared more about other people than I did about myself.

After being broken and confused to the point it had me asking myself, *How in the hell did I get here?* This is when I just knew I had to do something, and fast. Operating as if everything was fine and carrying on while my life truly was an emotional wreck could not continue. I still didn't understand what I needed in order to live a healthy and fruitful life, but I knew I was mentally, physically and emotionally drained.

When anything becomes drained, there is nothing more to give. It can no longer operate as it was originally intended, and the basic act of functioning becomes limited. When something operates with a limited capacity, you truly do not know what you're going to get from it, if anything. You may get a smile and a happy person today and tomorrow, you could get a completely different person. At that point in my life, I felt exhausted. I disconnected from everything important. When something is disconnected, there is no power, no function, and you're left to continue while in survival mode. I became both selfless and selfish. What others needed didn't really matter at all to me, because this was all about me and how I was feeling. Self-preservation was my only recourse. Being drained from life's unexpected blows, I found myself only concerned about self.

I finally thought I'd figured it out, after years of searching and discontent. What I needed was to admit to myself exactly where I was and that something was wrong within *me*. Almost like a person in recovery from an addiction of some sort that needed a recovery program. But that led me to ask myself, "Do I have an addiction?" Because if I need recovery, then I probably had an addiction.

I researched the word *addiction* to make sure I wasn't being crazy. Merriam-Webster defines addiction as "the condition of being addicted to a particular substance." So, I asked myself, *Okay, I don't do drugs of any kind, so this cannot apply to me, right?* I kept reading and saw "thing or activity." As I read a bit further, it listed synonyms of the word addiction, and they were "dependent, dependency, habit." I'm thinking, okay, this is a joke, because I'm one of the most independent people that I know. And the very last word—*habit*—stuck out like a sore thumb. Was I addicted to a habit or habits?

As people we tend to think of drugs and alcohol, or demeaning activities, when we talk about addiction. But the fact of the matter is we can be addicted to things we do every day and not even realize it. Working out, eating, shopping, video games can all be addictions. We could even be addicted to people. Addictions are the chase of some high that we will never receive again, which directly correlates to something we are missing or covering up.

By now, I was addicted to myself. What made me and me alone happy... A sense of entitlement, arrogance, and fuck the whole world mentality. Somewhat of a narcissistic-minded person. Typically, they are smart individuals who are passionate, have strong work ethic, and some even tend to be leaders in the workplace. But all have an inflated image of self that negatively impacts every person they meet. They ultimately lose or never cultivate positive relationships without changing their behavior. I had to learn to identify, admit and be honest with myself about who I was before any positive changes could happen.

"Gassing myself up so I never have to deal with low self-esteem again"

The Ultimate Loss

I am all too familiar with the feeling of loss.
Loss has broken me into so many pieces that the
average person could not fathom the effects or see
the scars, which had crept into various areas of my
life. As I reflect back, I mean, when I thought I was
at my lowest, cut so deep and fallen so hard, the
thought of recovery was far into the abyss. Loss has
a way of changing you in a fashion that you not
know who you are, or the people around you. Who
you once were perceived to be does no longer exist
and who you've become is a total stranger. Loss
never returns you to your original state of being, but
it can give you a renewed mind, and a different
outlook on life as it is.

*Just think for two minutes, of the worst news
you could ever receive, what would that be? Ponder
that and embrace every emotion possible.*

Family. Almost everyone has suffered a loss of
a loved one—a family member, a friend, even a pet.
Some relationships are stronger than others; the
bonds that are created by two people truly define
the magnitude or the significance of the
relationship. Some connections and instances that
develop within people can impact our lives in many
ways and for an undetermined amount of time. Of
all the relationships we have, family is the most
significant. These relationships were created to be a
group of people by default. We don't get to select
our family members but we do get to decide who
we choose to procreate family with. Family cannot
be changed, but the nature of the relationships can

be altered. Sometimes even bonds with people you meet in life can be so strong that you feel the person is like family. The love and connections between people can be so amazing, that the thought of losing them….is enough. Challenges and events can obliquely change the dynamics of any relationship.

Every family has problems and mine certainly wasn't perfect... My family's structure and how we operated was a bit unorthodox. While someone from afar may say we seem distant or unattached or have a difficult way of expressing love. One's assessment would be accurate. The only thing that truly matters is we understand and love in a peculiar way. Our differences in personalities still never outweighed our similarities. I was smart, feisty, bold yet somewhat of a loner and always found a way to get into trivial troubles. I often think it was because I was always bored and easily distracted. I wasn't afraid of much of anything, loved to have fun but enjoyed being alone *rather than* with a group most times. My middle sister was intelligent and sharp with a strong personality. She was the math and science expert amongst us. I absolutely despised science and math and if I could get rid of it, I probably would; however, she excelled in those subjects and enjoyed it. My oldest sister was extremely outgoing, smart, and had a free spirit. She seemed to know everyone and lived life on the surface. Patently, we are all still the same today.

My brother was laid back, yet challenging and naïve. He was overly protective as well, even though he was the youngest sibling and desired to be the oldest most the time. He had issues though…we all had issues. Or, was it that God created four unique individuals from the same parents with massively different personalities, mindsets, and thoughts about how life should really be? After all, being different is what provides character and a unique sense of self. Much of our parents' attributes were passed down to us, as it shaped us into four completely different people who had their own ideas, ultimately moving us toward different directions in life.

My parents married and divorced when my siblings and I were very young. As a child this was my first encounter with loss. Losing my father's presence in the home at such a young age contributed to my behavior with several of my encounters with people over time.

I was just five years old and my brother was under a year old when my mother gathered me and my three siblings to take a train ride and moved to the Midwest. I didn't fully understand what was happening, but I knew things were quite different, as we were in a different place and someone important in my life was not there. The most integral piece to the family puzzle was missing…my father. After failed attempts at mending the relationship, a tough divorce and separation was in the foreseeable future.

As a little girl, I thought my father was awesome. We were very spoiled children and there was very little need for discipline from my father because we knew whatever he said, he meant. I thought he was cool and popular because he had a lot of friends and loved to have a good time. He used to take me on motorcycle rides when my sisters were at school. With encouragement he would say, "Grab the handle bars and give it some gas!" He taught me how to stop the motorcycle and how to change the gears. He made me feel as if I was really driving the motorcycle.

My father provided and protected but he didn't understand the meaning of protecting us from himself. I learned many life lessons from my father that I will never forget. He wasn't aware of the lessons he indirectly was teaching me, about relationships, having a supportive partner and love. Alcoholism, infidelities, and a secondary lifestyle resulting in a separation was inevitable.

While my siblings and I never wanted for anything, my mother was a homemaker. She stayed home with us when we were young until we were old enough to be independent. My mother's ability to take care of the children and the house was truly amazing and a blessing. A great cook, a hairdresser, proper etiquette at the dinner table and ensuring we had a strong spiritual background. Yes, my mother did that. I learned my role inside the home from my mother.

I learned at a young age what loyalty, mental stability and an ability to resolve disputes by inadvertently watching my parents function through disloyalty, mental instability and the inability to resolve disputes in a healthy manner and what I didn't learn was how to take care of my emotions, hot to love myself and that I have value.

The universe dealt me the worse hand ever. I lost my grandmother—the backbone of my family, my prayer warrior, my voice of reason. She was as close to a saint that I'd ever seen. She was a comedian and had a way of finding humor in all situations.

My grandmother was a very special woman to me. At times she was a woman of very few words and other times…you couldn't wait for her to finish talking about her thoughts. She was a devout Christian and she wanted to live the life of a Christian woman more than talk about it. She always had a story to tell. Some of those stories she would tell over and over again because she wanted it to be engrained in you... There was a lesson in every conversation with her.

Many of those stories were true to life while a few of them turned into jokes somehow. Overcoming adversity and being resilient were two characteristics she embodied. I once came outside for gym class in elementary school, my classmates and I were lining up on the front lawn for class; where gym class was often held. I look to the far right and I see my grandmother. She loved having garage sales whenever she could. She enjoyed thrifting, buying and selling antiques. She could spot things of value from a mile away and many things people would pass up, she would stop for

That day she had a spread of items across the school lawn with a sign reading, "Garage Sale Today." She managed to get the school to allow her to have a garage sale on the front lawn of the campus. She was one of the boldest people I've ever known and wasn't afraid of anything.

Not long after, I lost one of my favorite uncles. My uncle was a well put together man. You knew he was around because he had an infectious laugh; you could always hear him, before you could see him. He was tall, jovial and always had something to say. He usually had a quick comeback to any joke. I would often pause to hear his response.

People who knew him well called him Dino because he was so tall; he often had to duck going through doorways to avoid bumping his head. He often had a story or wanted to tell you about something he'd experienced in life. Many times those events weren't all that pleasant, but sometimes they were. If you were up for a good debate, he was your guy.

He knew a little bit about a lot of stuff. He introduced me to fried frog legs and taught me how to tie my shoes when I was 3 years old; all in the same day. I will never forget those special moments. I often think he just wanted people to understand where he was coming from. It seemed he was doing that a lot, like he was always trying to get someone to listen, trying to prove himself or maybe he just wanted to be accepted for who he was. I identify with some of the same characteristics of my grandmother and my uncle.

And then my brother…I lost my one and only brother on my birthday. Every year when I add another year to my life, I remind myself that he is no longer here to share another year with me. The memory of that moment, when I heard the life-

30

changing news of losing my brother, still replays in my head. It was the day before my birthday, the angst and eagerness of my big day was approaching. The day before my birthday, I was at work - excited, surfing social media, opening my Facebook platform. There was a message in my inbox. Who else but my one and only brother?

I opened the message with anticipation but at the same time with one eye closed. When it came to my brother, I never knew what I was going to get. The message read, *Happy birthday sister. I love you.*

I replied, *Thank you but you know today is not my birthday.* That would be the last time I heard from my brother. I never received a reply. The next morning, I was awakened at 5:00 a.m. with a call from my father. I automatically assumed he was calling to be the first to wish me a happy birthday. My life would forever be changed.

My brother meant everything to me—and when I say everything, I mean *everything.* I kept my phone on just in case my brother would call me from jail or if he'd ran out of gas an hour away, expecting me to come get him (and I would, of course). I made extra keys to my house so I could leave a set under the doormat just in case he came to my house unexpectedly. He was full of surprises. His personal struggles, compiled with the challenges of this world, eventually led him to succumb, and he was gone. I envied my brother's arrival and mourned his departure.

And then…my father. The man I hated but grew

to love. I forgave him for his shortfalls in the past, and we became good friends. His phone calls increased from only the weekends to everyday, until sometimes I was greeted with a few calls per day. I thought he was just bored at work. And then one day he was gone. I feel as if my life literally stopped for two straight years. I was in neutral, completely out of body, out of focus, off course, out of space and distant.

This shit hurt. While going through the emotional trauma of losing family, I was expected to carry on with my life as if nothing ever happened. The clock will keep ticking and there is nothing I can do to stop it. At least that's what I thought. How does one continue on with life after a traumatic life changing event?

With little time to recover and never truly mourning the loss of my immediate family members, I still had to uphold the responsibilities of being a mother, a student, a sister, an employee, a boss, a friend, and a girlfriend. All the things I had to be for the good of others and not taking care of myself. I'd lost my identity and had no idea who I was. Merely existing - more like surviving. I was present for everybody else, except myself. The basic needs to provide and care for myself inside and out lacked cultivation. I was unable to do this and almost in denial of my behavior.

"Healing is ongoing, and losing control is up to you."

If you have experienced or are now experiencing an event you would consider to be an ultimate loss, where are you now with the acceptance of those events you had no control over? Has it been difficult to get past? Is it causing other disruptions in your day to day life?

Accepting what we cannot change is part of recovering and turning our negative emotions into useful energy. Learning to accept that I could not change the events, allowed the space for me to grow through the loss. It also provides the leverage of learning to control emotions even when we do not understand the details. Emotions should not have the authority to control anyone, merely help to identify the difference between pleasure and pain.

Self-Discovery

That Saturday I decided to go for a quick morning breakfast. I pulled into the parking lot and noticed the place was completely packed, but that didn't matter to me because I wanted breakfast. I hurried through the door; put my name on the long list of guests waiting to be seated. I knew I had time to waste and I advised the waitress I was going to the restroom quickly; in the event my name was called as I stepped away. Gone just 5 minutes, I return and I took a seat. Patiently I waited for my name to be called, I looked around at the people who had not yet been seated, and I recognized five sets of customers who came in after me had been called. I found the host and asked her what happened.

She said she called my name and I replied, "Ma'am, you knew I went to the restroom. Are you kidding me?"

She seated me expeditiously, silently acknowledging my demanding question. While waiting, I briefly surfed the internet and began to pan the restaurant. I noticed a guy sitting next to me, also waiting while on a FaceTime call with a friend, loudly discussing his Friday night episodes with women. To my right, a preteen and her father sat at a table for what was probably an early Father's Day celebration, and they were both glued to their phones. The father looked unbothered; his daughter seemed disgusted as if she didn't want to be there.

I looked to my left and noticed two men staring at me while their wives were on the opposite sides of the table engaged in conversation. Next to the men was a family of four—two women and two little girls. The eldest woman expressed her frustrations with the waitress about the hot sauce on the table. And the family of five immediately next to their table had a family member who was disabled, receiving less than subpar attention from everyone else.

What I observed was people, their behaviors, how everyone is different—and at the same time I made assumptions about each of the groups. I didn't know any of the people in the restaurant, but after briefly watching all of them, I prejudged each one in a matter of minutes. We as people do that quite easily. Judgement is easy when it's delivered rather than received.

Understand that no two people were ever created the same - thanks to God. We all have different ideas, methods, attitudes, behaviors, thoughts, and opinions that make us unique. One lesson on my journey to winning was that I had to learn to accept and not judge people for whom they are. For one, everyone wants to be accepted and no one wants to be judged. This is a very difficult concept for most people, including myself.

I found myself judging people quite often. What I learned about myself and my judging is that I couldn't stand to be judged. As much constructive criticism as I dish out on a regular basis with family, friends, and mostly at work, I hadn't come to accept it from others. There's a difference between constructive criticism and judging, however, both forms of feedback require an individual to be confident and have self-esteem, which I lacked.

What was it about myself that I just couldn't stand the thought of receiving negative feedback from someone else, yet I easily dished it out? What did I think I was lacking? Or was I afraid that what was said to me was actually true, which ultimately would put me in a position to alter or change something about myself? I despised change imposed from anyone but myself. How dare someone tell me that something is wrong with me and that I need to make changes or else! The arrogance and feistiness in me almost always surfaced, and quite often the scenario never ended on a good note. With no sense of self-identity, searching to understand who I was became a separate journey and I had no idea where I should start.

Eventually I dissected the meaning of the words *self* and *identify*. *Self* being I and everything that is in me, internal and external; my personality and how I connect with others; my genetic makeup; my family tree.

Identity being what I represent; what I stand for; how I see myself amongst my family, peers, co-workers, and others that live in this world; and how I want the world to see me. My reflection to the earth, my after scent…how will people remember me? I had no idea.

Learning who I was became a process that

required homework, research, and time alone to self-reflect. I read many self-help books, paid a lot of money at seminars, sought professional help from counselors, and had countless chats with girlfriends over cocktails while ranting about things I could control and could not control. Searching to find, or define, who I was based off the opinions of others.

On the uphill to my prime, in search of me, I struggled for many years. I learned that knowing and understanding who I am takes a lifetime but understanding where I was in life and who I was at this place in time was important. I struggled with my own self-image and had to first understand why I was struggling. The first step was to take responsibility for myself and my actions, realizing controlled and uncontrolled situations. *Separating the controlled from the uncontrolled.*

We can only control our actions and reactions. Simply put, it's how we act and how we respond to the elements on Earth. And how we react is directly related to our thoughts and emotions, which are two factors we control. Without having control of these two outputs, we can become extremely emotionally unstable and unpredictable.

When we look at self-identity, things we cannot control are automatically removed. As we go back to Chapter Five, the loss of my family members was the only event I could not control. Everything else mentioned thereafter was all in my control. Uncontrolled factors are those that only God has control over. Understanding and respecting this is key in defining what we can and cannot control or change in our lives. I could not control the loss or order of the events of losing my family members. None of us want to bear these crosses and burdens no matter what stages or times in our lives they arise. However, beyond the stage of grieving, we have full control over how we respond. We are responsible for our actions no matter what challenges we face in life.

"When you can't control the situation, take control of your response."

Recovery

I. Know Your Triggers

Most of us have a line where if anyone crosses it, you better turn off all the lights because the party is over. What makes you tick? What pisses you off? What gets under your skin to the point it would set you off in a New York second? These are *triggers*. Knowing your triggers is half the battle in knowing what you allow and how you respond. Our responses can alter the outcomes of a situation if they are not accepted by the receiver.

For me, when someone rejected my advances, I immediately became offended. Being rejected can appear in many forms. Not getting a job, plans not going the way I envisioned, my ideas in a meeting not being selected for a project. In situations like these, I found myself reacting in an immature manner rather than accept that everything will not always go the way I would like.

I also had a feeling that I was no longer in control when things did not go my way. Not having control for me was not about wanting to dictate and manage other people, but the fear of not knowing the outcome for myself. What type of situation will this decision I am a part of put me in? If I could not answer this question for myself, I responded. I had to work really hard when these moments would arise, when I found myself about to respond to the rejection. This was a mental game I had to play with myself. I had to slow down and process what I was hearing from the sender. I failed countless times

43

with this exercise before I finally got it right. I learned a few things when I actually slowed down.

Another trigger for me was when someone lied to me. The thought of someone not telling me the truth caused me to act out in various ways. What I needed to understand was that I was not the one who lied or decided to be untruthful. This was another person's decision to not be truthful. This decision had nothing to do with me at all; I just happened to be the recipient. I had to decide that I would not allow someone else's unhealthy truths to affect me in a way, which resulted in outwardly expressing myself.

Some of the things I learned when interacting with others:

1. I learned the sender was going in a completely different direction than what I had intended in the beginning. Had I not stopped to listen I could have ruined a great outcome by responding too fast.
2. I learned that once some people figured out what button to push, they would try to push it every time. When people learn what upsets you or what makes you tick, they sometimes get a rise from seeing you act out. Don't waste your time with people like this.
3. I learned that, by slowing down, I might actually understand something by saying less in certain situations.

What are some of your triggers, and what happens in the moment that you feel you are losing control of a situation?

_____
_____
_____
_____
_____
_____
_____
_____
_____
_____
_____
_____

II. Stages of Loss

The biggest take away from losing is the unexpected sacrifices we must make. Having to make a sacrifice is enough in and of itself because nobody ever wants to be the bearer of the cross. This can make one feel as if they have no choice. It was like I was being forced to move from where I was mentally, physically, and emotionally. *But for what?* I asked myself. I was comfortable, and comfort has a way of making us feel safe and protected but limits our abilities to grow. And further, being safe and protected prevented me from being hurt—at least in theory. But what I didn't know at the time was the importance of losing is necessary in order to win. Losing teaches us many things that can take our future to new heights.

First, we must go through the stages of losing:

A. **Experience the loss and losing the emotions connected to the separation of familiarity.** This is the most difficult part of the loss stage. Losing family, losing a job, or something as simple as losing a shoe—dealing with separating from anything you are familiar with is not going to be easy.

B. **Acceptance.** Accepting that which is lost. I cannot change, alter, or make it return. I must accept the fact I could not change anything that I lost whether it is any fault of my own or divine intervention. This does not mean wallowing in loss but getting past the loss itself and accepting that this is the way it is and there is nothing I can do to change the situation; I can only change the way I see the situation.

C. **Gratitude.** Being grateful helps us through the acceptance process. Remembering the good times I had before the loss of every situation helped me to move forward. Remembering the good and the benefits that job brought before you lost it, or the good times you shared with a loved one before losing them, helps you go through the acceptance step in the stages of losing.

D. **Forgiveness.** Relieve yourself of false guilt, blame or shame and any offenses, making way for opening your heart and mind to new beginnings.

Draw your focus here:

1. Without loss, there are no true lessons. Without loss, there is nothing to be learned. Losing has a way of forcing us to practice a task over and over again. How many shots did Michael Jordan miss, or how many races did Jackie Joyner Kersey lose? Practicing to lose without the expectation of winning creates an expert by accident, one that will never be forgotten.

2. Losing challenges us to move on or move forward. When something no longer serves us the way we want to be served, the feeling of loss or defeat eventually causes us to move on. What we can't control is the time it will take us to heal from the loss, but time (as we know) heals all wounds and moving on is necessary. Without moving on, new opportunities will never happen. We will never know what lies ahead or what new doors can open for us.

3. Losing builds character. Looking back over the process - the strength, determination, and growth that is developed in a person builds character that would not have come without the challenge of loss in life.

4. Loss teaches us how to deal with life on life's terms, blessing us with the choice to face it rather than feel defeated with the challenges that are attached to it.

III. Positioned to Win

Facing obstacles provides us with an opportunity to position ourselves and overcome rather than just accept defeat.

In order to position yourself to win, you must focus on enduring instead of whether you will win or lose. Stay in the game until it's over, no matter what the result may be. Even if your situation looks as if you're going to lose, proper positioning prevents premature losses. What is a premature loss, one might ask? Losing something in its infancy stage, before it has an opportunity to grow. Self-doubt, esteem deficiencies and not knowing who you are can create premature losses.

Throughout my many stages of loss, one thing I learned (after identifying and accepting the losses and preparing myself to overcome) is the recognition that I had not fully healed. At times I found myself replaying or rehearsing some of the same steps repeatedly in my head. I had not completely graduated to overcoming with every situation. I constantly battled with depression at many intervals.

In the first chapter you may recall that I acknowledged there were areas of my life where I still felt broken and felt I would forever be broken.

What I learned from this did not mean I could not overcome and win - even when struggling in my brokenness. I could still operate in success and still be broken. I recognized it was in the back and forth that propelled me forward. It was while I was

48

juggling depression with one issue and healing with another that I was still growing.

I learned there was not a definitive time frame of how long I would be in any one stage, in each situation. As I healed in struggling with my weight loss, I was still broken in dealing with the loss of my family members and subsequently, other challenges arrived that I was not prepared to deal with.

In moving forward and positioning yourself to win, there are four things that can help:

1. Know who you are
2. Set boundaries
3. Have self-control
4. Have standards

Positioning myself to win was the hardest step, because this was the stage of self-care. This was the stage I had to stop making excuses and start making improvements.

Know Who You Are

Knowing who you are can mean identifying your strengths and your weaknesses, having morals and value, or knowing your likes and dislikes. Ask yourself, what do I want for myself? What am I good at? Where can I use improvement? Truly knowing yourself is a precursor to setting boundaries, without knowing yourself, it's impossible to set boundaries.

Know who you are: List some of your morals and values here. Mention some of your likes and dislikes and things that are non-negotiable to you.

_____

_____

_____

_____

_____

_____

Set Boundaries

Saying what you mean and meaning what you say. When deciding about something that affects your life, be willing to stick to your decision. Do not allow what someone else is doing to change your mind. This is an area you can afford to waver.

When saying no, I had to mean it. Understanding that not accepting defeat was not the same as accepting I was broken and that I still dealt with depression—but that I would not fall deep into the depths of a situation or circumstance, allowing myself to be put in a position where I needed a life jacket to pull myself out. Set boundaries mentally, physically, and emotionally.

In preparation to winning, what are some boundaries that you need to set for yourself?

_____

_____

_____

_____

_____

Self-Control

Understanding your limits, your triggers and creating balance leads to self-control. If I struggle with alcoholism or gambling, going to a bar or to the casino would be triggers for me. Sometimes things and people we attach ourselves to can be toxic and become triggers that prevent us from having self-control. If we are not in control in that area, we are not able to win moving forward when these obstacles present themselves. Triggers are setbacks and are signs of not having control.

What are some areas in your life that need streamlining?

_____

_____

_____

_____

_____

Standards

Having standards means maintaining a level of quality in areas that matter the most to your future, your being and your overall success. Standards say: I will only allow these types of people to be in my inner circle, or I will only date this man/woman possessing these characteristics. Setting standards prevents us from several things. One is settling. Settling has a lot to do with how we feel about ourselves. Sometimes one may not think they deserve something better than what they have, or what they have is the best there is, but is it? Knowing what you want allows you to set standards. If we do not know what we truly want, how can we set any kind of standard?

What are some areas that you need to set standards? Is it with friends, at work, or while dating? List some of those standards here.

_____

_____

_____

_____

_____

_____

Experiencing many stages of loss, I learned what I was really made of. . I no longer had to pretend or be the person the world dictated me to me. I could freely be happy with the fact that I was not perfect, and it was through my imperfections that I became the best version of myself. I realized that when God created me, he only made one of me in His image—and that alone was plenty.

Loss can take us on an unexpected journey we never imagined. One thing I've learned is some things you never completely heal from and some things you do... I learned that healing and self-love is a continual process. As we grow as individuals, shedding the layers of life are endless and we are constantly on God's potter's wheel to become who He created us to be. I've also learned that we never *arrive*, if we are always working to become better than we were yesterday.

On the road to emerging, it's necessary to maintain balance during the breaking process, which essentially helps us sustain throughout the healing and building stage. To become who our Creator predestined us to be, a strong foundation must be built. How do we build a strong foundation? Through trials, tribulations and tests. Without test, trials & tribulations, how will one truly know what they're made of? I made it....I made it to the stage of understanding my identity through some of the most impactful experiences in life; loss, love, and pain

My experiences have taught me how to love myself. Love myself to the deepest level there possibly could be. The good and the bad. The things that someone else may love, I may raise my middle finger to, because what I learned is this is about me and my foundation. And if I don't have my own foundation - every circumstance I am approached with could destroy me. Loving myself means rejecting any and everything that doesn't serve me well. People, situations and things. The ability to distinguish positive and negative influences is fundamentally necessary.

It is important to never accept a mediocre version of yourself. God created every one of us for greatness. To live at the highest level of our potential, living a well enough life does not allow you to do these three things:

1. Live an impactful lifestyle
2. Create a legacy
3. Learn who you truly are

Living an impactful life connects you with other people. Our lives should touch others and help other people become the best version of themselves. What I learned throughout my many challenges was my destiny, or life is directly tied to someone else's success and that in turn makes me successful. Someone else needs you and in order to be that divine connection for someone else, it's important to not accept an okay or well enough lifestyle. It is imperative to be healthy, mindful and mentally intact in order to be the necessary key to unlock the giant within someone else.

Being mentally available, allows us to tap into that purpose and have the ability to discern and see the needs of others and not just yourself. Having the capacity to pour into the next person, being able to help someone else reveal their purpose, can be an integral part of their ultimate success and essentially tied to your legacy. Your legacy is how people will remember you. Did you do anything impactful while you were here on earth? Whose life did you help to change?

Emotional health and wellness are required in order to be a bridge, helping to carry someone else across to where they need to be in life. And without it, can cause devastation to someone else's life. The theory six degrees of separation, says we are all connected by six connections or less from one another. This theory can suggest we are all connected and should be.

My goal was to push and no longer be just okay with my achievements in life, but work to understand how I could become a better, healthier Sharee. My ultimate success is to become who God predestined me to be - Mind, Body & Spirit. Mediocrity of "well enough" can keep us from reaching that destination. I could no longer use what happened to me as a child, the loss of my loved ones or the experiences from failed relationships, negative connections or life's challenges, as a crutch or an excuse for failure.

I could no longer use losing my loved ones as an excuse to function at less than best and no longer an excuse and accept what the world handed me, but to rise above my challenges. Rising above the challenges helped me to build my character. I was blessed to learn what I liked and what I didn't like. I grew to learn who I was beneath the surface; the real me. Rising above my challenges helped me gain understanding as to why I experienced some things at the levels I did. Mediocrity can cause one to make excuses for the unacceptable and never be held accountable for their own behavior.

Mediocrity will never allow one to seek to find, search to discover, or desire to want to know who they truly are.......your hidden value.

If you enjoyed this book, then I ask you one small favor – would you be kind enough to leave a review for this book on Amazon?

I promise it will be quick and painless.

Thank you for sharing your time and supporting The Depth of Hidden Value!

Should you have any questions for me, please feel free to reach out at:

ssquaredbooks@gmail.com

Or visit my
Facebook @ Author Sharee Strickland

Instagram @ intriguedbyeau

JOURNAL

_____

_____

_____

_____

_____

_____

_____

_____

_____

_____

_____

_____

_____

_____

_____

_____

_____

_____

_____

_____

_____

_____

_____

_____